BRITAIN IN OLD PHC   ..HS

AROUND
WITNEY
PAST & PRESENT

CHRIS MITCHELL &
LAURENCE WATERS

SUTTON PUBLISHING LIMITED

OXFORDSHIRE BOOKS

Sutton Publishing Limited
Phoenix Mill · Thrupp · Stroud
Gloucestershire · GL5 2BU

XFORDSHIRE BOOKS

First published 1998

Copyright © Chris Mitchell &
Laurence Waters, 1998

Title page photograph: Witney Church looking
north

British Library Cataloguing in Publication Data
A catalogue record for this book is available from the
British Library.

ISBN 0-7509-1896-9

Typeset in 10/12 Perpetua.
Typesetting and origination by
Sutton Publishing Limited.
Printed in Great Britain by
Ebenezer Baylis, Worcester.

This early photograph of children in the Market Square was produced by J.T. Bridgeman, portrait and
landscape photographer.

CONTENTS

Introduction   5

1. Cogges & Newland   7

2. Wood Green   17

3. West End & Bridge Street   25

4. Mill Street, Tower Hill & Burford Road   35

5. High Street   43

6. Market Square & the Butter Cross   61

7. Corn Street   75

8. Church Green   83

9. The Leys & Railway Station   93

10. The Villages & Towns Around Witney   101

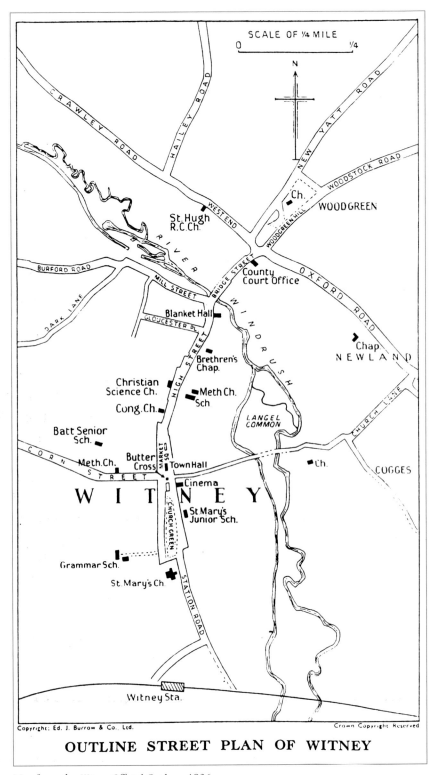

Map from the *Witney Official Guide, c. 1936.*

INTRODUCTION

To most people, the first mention of Witney is closely followed by the word 'blanket'. For hundreds of years the town has been associated with the manufacture of blankets which, so the story goes, are of such good quality because of the use of the waters of the River Windrush.

Few will mention or even know of the *Witteneye* which was the domain of the Bishops of Winchester during the early Middle Ages. It was one of the original towns represented in the Parliaments of Edward I, Edward II and Edward III and was used as a retreat for students at Oxford University who wished to escape the plague in the fifteenth and sixteenth centuries.

While the Witney of today attracts fewer people trying to escape the plague, it nevertheless thrives as a market town and a satellite dormitory area for Oxford. That is not to say that Witney is totally reliant on its more famous neighbour. Indeed, Witney has its own satellite towns and villages, like Bampton and Stanton Harcourt, which are also explored in this book.

Witney's industrial and commercial sectors have shown remarkable growth and diversification in recent times and the county's development plans show that Witney is expected to continue that growth well into the twenty-first century. In the twentieth century Witney has hosted two breweries, the ubiquitous blanket industry, an aerodrome which was vital to the war effort, food manufacturers, a car parts manufacturer and, more recently, a Formula 1 racing team. Witney is a town with great traditions which refuses to stand still. The medieval market town of *Witteneye* has come a long way.

History has given us many markers about the development of Witney from those early days but it is often difficult to visualise those changes. The invention of the camera gave us the ability to enjoy a different, more concrete view of social and economic development. We are also lucky that fashion dictated that the Edwardians sent and collected picture postcards to the point of obsession. Frequently these postcards are enriched further by the messages written on the back and, indeed, some of these messages have been used as the basis for the captions in this book. The mass production of these vistas and the *vignettes* inscribed on them provide a rich seam of historical document which has been tapped here.

By contrasting these early pictures with photographs taken today, *Around Witney Past & Present* gives us a much clearer vision of the town's progress this century than we can realistically have of the Witney of the Middle Ages. It will, we hope, also make people stop and consider the issues surrounding Witney's rapid growth. It is plain to today's visitor that the town is thriving and has an enjoyable bustle but at the same time the comparison of the crowded streets of today with the quieter streets of the past should give us food for thought.

We hope that the following pages will mean different things to different people. To those who lived and grew up in Witney, it will be a reminder of their childhood town. To those who have moved into the area, it will give them a better understanding of the town's heritage. To visitors, it will be a souvenir of their experiences. There is, though, another side to this book which makes us look at the way Witney has developed over the years and makes us ask where it is going.

The rich legacy of photographs and pictures contained here will give us and future generations a benchmark by which we can ensure that Witney never loses the character which makes it so well loved.

Children assemble on Church Green to celebrate King George V's Silver Jubilee in 1935.

CHAPTER ONE

COGGES & NEWLAND

Bottom of Oxford Hill, looking east into Newland.

Witney from the Oxford Road, 1920s. The road was much narrower then with steep banks and an abundance of mature trees. The telegraph poles on the left-hand side of the road provided the telephone service for Witney which was the start of modernisation for its inhabitants.

The approach to Witney as it is today. The trees have gone and the road has been widened to provide an entrance to Cogges, where a new development of houses has been built. The telegraph poles are long gone and have been replaced by modern street lighting and road markings.

Oxford Hill looking east, 1930s. The photograph shows a distinct lack of traffic, especially considering this was the main road between London and Wales.

Oxford Hill today, cluttered with cars. Most of the houses remain, with only modest updating. The presence of modern-day traffic was relieved by the building of a bypass around the town; this was opened in 1977.

Coggs Church
Witney

St Mary's Church, Cogges, *c.* 1910. Also shown is the vicarage which incorporates part of a small Benedictine Priory founded in 1103. The house dates back to the twelfth century only in part. The incumbent in 1915 when this photograph was taken was the Revd R. Hodgell. Cogges is mis-spelt, which was not unusual at the time.

Little has changed to disturb the peaceful scene. The bridge has been replaced by a more modern structure and Manor Farm is now Cogges Farm Museum, with the house restored and the animals returned.

An early view of the River Windrush, which flows through Witney and provided the motive power for the wool industry for which the town is famous. This is one of the two bridges that cross the Windrush on the route from Cogges to the town centre. It was used as a short cut to the railway station, in Station Lane, behind the church on Church Green.

Again, little has changed, and the spot is still a quiet refuge from the busy town.

Newland, looking towards Oxford Hill before the road was widened. There was a toll house on the left.

The road is now wider and straighter and buildings on both the left- and right-hand sides of the road have disappeared. Most of the changes have taken place on the left-hand side of the road, with new businesses appearing and vacant land being used for further development, mainly houses.

Newland from Church Lane, looking towards West End, with the Griffin public house standing out halfway down the left-hand side. The building on the right was Mr Dix's bakery.

Modernisation has provided pavements and the extensive development of the right-hand side of the road but the Griffin remains.

Newland closer to West End, *c.* 1910. Children pose for the photographer; their Edwardian dress typifies the period. In the distance a horse and cart can be seen close to the premises now occupied by Fifield and Son. The firm started its business in the 1930s as motor car proprietors, offering Austin motor hearses and limousines for hire.

The children have disappeared and, unusually, only one vehicle appears in the picture. Only minor changes can be seen to the houses. Fifield and Son remains and continues to run a business from the same location.

Newland from West End, *c.* 1900. The building on the immediate right, Newland House, was adjacent to Newland Mill. The area on the left of the road had still to be developed.

Newland Mill has long since disappeared and its buildings have been replaced by a housing development. The property on the main road, Newland House, once the home of Charles Early, is now a nursing home. Opposite is the Pensclose development.

The junction of Newland, Wood Green Hill, West End and Bridge Street, *c.* 1910. The building on the extreme left, now called Staple Hall, was originally a coaching inn. In the centre is the Court Inn.

The junction today. Part of Staple Hall has been demolished to allow widening of the road and it is now a nursing home. The Court Inn continues to flourish and mini-roundabouts have been added to this busy junction.

CHAPTER TWO

WOOD GREEN

Holy Trinity Church, Wood Green.

Wood Green from Narrow Hill, with a glimpse down New Yatt Road. Mature trees obscure the green on the right. This green was used as the starting and judging point for the Witney carnival parade in the 1930s.

Narrow Hill as it is today. Pavements have been introduced, and behind the houses on the left there is extensive housing development in the Farmers Close area (building commenced in the late 1960s). Towards the green, the trees have been thinned out to reveal more houses.

Another view of Wood Green featuring Holy Trinity Church, *c*. 1920. The church was built in 1849 and was partly funded by public subscription. The pulpit and screen for it were made by H. Shuffrey, who had premises on Church Green. The church is surrounded by an open area known as the green which has always been a favourite spot for recreation.

The church today occupies an only superficially changed setting, still with plenty of safe playing space bordered by spreading trees.

Wood Green from the Three Pigeons public house. In this view of the elegant setting, mature trees line the road and green.

The houses as they are today. In the distance new development in Woodstock Road can be seen. Changes have been made to accommodate the motor car.

More of the fine Georgian town houses of Witney which surround the green. On the left is The Gables.

Some of the large trees have disappeared and pavements and street lighting have been introduced. The house at the end of the road is no longer a private residence and now provides offices for the West Oxfordshire District Council.

Woodstock Road from Wood Green, 1910. There was virtually no development on the left-hand side of the road at this time.

Today's view shows how much the left-hand side of the road has been developed. The right-hand side saw change in the 1950s and 1960s when Wood Green school was built.

Further along Woodstock Road, 1915.

The trees have matured to such an extent that they now dominate the road. The area to the left, out of the picture, has been significantly developed, and housing occupies the land between Woodstock Road and New Yatt Road.

An early twentieth-century view of the north side of Woodstock Road as it leaves the town. There is little evidence of development on the left-hand side.

The passing years have left few visible marks on the buildings.

CHAPTER THREE

WEST END &
BRIDGE STREET

Bridge Street, Witney, looking north.

West End looking towards Crawley, *c.* 1900. This was an important route in and out of Witney. At the bottom of the road on the right was a toll house. Towards the town there were a number of businesses and a school, which have not survived the present day.

At first glance it would appear that very little about the buildings has changed. Some have been modernised but the character of the road is the same. A number of new businesses have sprung up close to the junction of Bridge Street and Narrow Hill.

The far end of West End, c. 1940. The prominent building on the right is the toll house. Around the corner and to the left towards Crawley is Smith's Crawley Mill, which formed an important part of the Witney blanket industry.

Changes are quite difficult to detect, although there has been significant development behind the houses on the right. A number of small businesses have also sprung up but alas Smith's Crawley Mill is long gone. The building is now a small industrial complex housing a number of businesses.

Bridge Street, looking towards Wood Green Hill, *c.* 1920. The photograph shows a group of men outside Middleton's gentlemen's outfitters at 24 Bridge Street. Later the shop passed into the hands of Cook and Boggis, cash drapers. It is now part of the Court Inn.

Bridge Street is awash with traffic today. On the right is the former County Court office which more recently housed the Department of Health and Social Security. The building next to it was formerly the Black Head Inn, and is now a private residence.

Another view of Bridge Street, this time showing Walker's newsagents at no. 15; Walker's published this photograph. They also sold stationery and tobacco. One of the billboards outside the shop reads 'Cabinet Split over Egypt'.

The premises are still occupied by a newsagent today, although the façade has been modernised and the billboards announce different crises.

Bridge Street, looking towards West End, *c.* 1900. The houses on the immediate right were demolished to extend Smith's Bridge Street Mill.

The prominent building on the right is the former Smith's Bridge Street Mill, which has now fallen into disuse. On the left is Wilkins garage; beyond, the private dwellings have been altered and are now Wesley Barrell's furniture store.

This view shows the original bridge before it was widened. The original bridge had three arches and was erected in 1822. It was altered in 1926 and again in the 1960s.

The bridge before it was altered, looking north down Bridge Street.

This view clearly shows how the road was improved by the bridge alterations.

New Bridge, complete with ornamental lighting and railings, was not only widened but the hump which was originally at the centre of the bridge was also significantly reduced. On the right, behind the cart, were the premises of James Marriott, coal, coke, anthracite and salt factors. This image is from around 1910.

Bridge Street as it is today. The junction has been altered and a mini roundabout added. Marriott's occupied the building on the immediate right until recently.

The River Windrush being used for recreation. Several of the large houses on Church Green and High Street had gardens that ran down to the river.

The scene today still offers the same temptations.

CHAPTER FOUR

MILL STREET, TOWER HILL & BURFORD ROAD

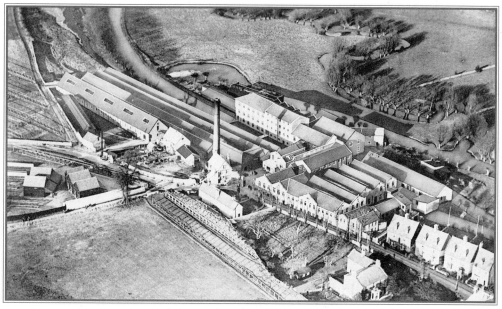

An aerial view of Early's Mill, Bridge Street.

Mill Street looking from the bridge. The road runs towards Burford Road. Beyond is Tower Hill, *c.* 1915.

Today's row of houses needs only the watchful children to be almost identical.

Mill Street looking east, c. 1920. The gas lighting dominates this picture. In the distance are the buildings and chimneys of the Charles Early Mill. The house railings disappeared to aid the war effort during the Second World War.

Although the Charles Early Mill remains, production of blankets has been transferred to the new premises further up the road. Queen Elizabeth II visited the new mills in April 1959.

A view of Early's Mill from Dark Lane, 1940.

Dark Lane as it is today. The quiet lane has become a proper thoroughfare, with the road layout remodelled and new buildings on both sides.

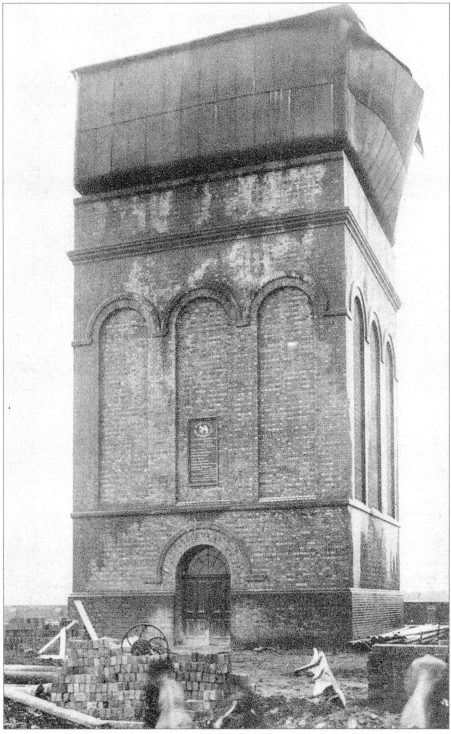

The water tower at the top of Tower Hill. It was opened in 1903, and burst in 1904 and again shortly afterwards. This had a devastating effect on the properties nearby: the Witney Union (workhouse) and house next door were flooded.

The water tower undergoing repairs.

The tower has long since gone and the site is filled with modern housing.

The entrance gates to the Witney Union (workhouse), Tower Hill, which was erected in 1835–6 and demolished in 1986. The workhouse was a large stone building with a detached chapel capable of housing 450 inmates. Its staff included a master, chaplain, medical officer and matron. In later years the building became Crawford's (collet making works).

The Witney Union site as it is today. Part of the original building (believed to be the chapel) can just be seen behind the trees on the left. Modern houses replace some of the buildings previously on the site – and the road is aptly called Union Way.

The aerodrome on Burford Road was used during both the First and Second World Wars. The aircraft pictured are de Havillands. The firm had a factory on the site in 1940.

The aircraft are long gone. The site was later occupied by Smith's, manufacturers of car components, mainly heaters, and this company has remained there.

CHAPTER FIVE

HIGH STREET

High Street, looking north.

E.A. Long's cart, wagon and cycle works at 108–10 High Street, adjacent to the bridge, *c.* 1900. The firm hired out cycles, and were also agents and certified repairers for Humber, Singer, Swift, Rover, Sparlbrook, Mohawk and Calcott bicycles.

Mike Wheeler, motorcycle dealer, occupies the premises today – so the cycle business has been carried out on these premises for nearly 100 years.

The western end of High Street showing the bridge and Blanket Hall, *c.* 1910. On the immediate right (barely visible) is the Plough Inn. Behind the cart is Blanket Hall, which was built in 1710 to weigh, measure and market the blankets manufactured in the area. It was noted for its single-handed clock. Just a couple of doors away from the Plough is the King's Arms.

The buildings on the right beyond Blanket Hall have been converted into commercial premises and house the Furnishing Centre. Opposite, behind the road sign, an entrance has been formed to an area called the Old Coachyard. The Plough Inn survives, but the King's Arms is now shops.

Staff pose for a photograph at Matilda Wiggins' shop at the western end of High Street (no. 92), *c.* 1910. She was a china and glass dealer and fellmonger, selling dressed animal skins and hides.

The premises today. They have been converted into homes and offices.

Gloucester Place, looking towards the High Street, 1899. In the centre of the photograph are the premises of Caleb Viner at 81 High Street. He was a grocer who also had another shop in High Street.

The scene is almost unchanged today. Stone and brick walls replace wooden palings.

High Street from Gloucester Place, 1920s. Although the photograph shows little traffic, plenty of the shops which exist to the present day can be seen. The trees at this end of the High Street have long since disappeared.

H. Berry's small family bakers at 86 High Street was pulled down in 1986 to make way for the new link road, which was opened in 1987. This new road (Witan Way) is clearly shown in this photograph; it has played an important part in the recent development of the town centre.

C. Osborn Tite, 58–60 High Street, 1890s. The shop sold ladies' and gentlemen's clothing. The business was founded in 1882 and remained until 1976.

The building remains but there have been significant alterations to the frontage, with a shopping area called Waterloo Walk created through the centre.

High Street looking towards Welch Way, relatively busy with traffic and shoppers, late 1940s. On the immediate right is Sidney Collis's shop at 61 High Street. He was a confectioner.

Much of the charm of the High Street has been retained over the last fifty years.

The High Street from Welch Way, 1918. On the left is Henry Long and Sons, ironmongers, with goods displayed on the pavement. Long had premises at 69 and 85 High Street.

Today the shops have been modernised but the broad footpaths remain, with the addition of traffic calming measures to tame vehicles. Regrettably, Henry Long no longer trades in the High Street.

High Street in the mid-1920s is an empty place.

The street has changed to provide access to Welch Way, the construction of which started in the 1960s.

The Methodist church and school, although the postcard is entitled the 'Wesleyan Chapel', *c.* 1910. The Wesleyan Mixed School, which was behind the church, was erected in 1855 and enlarged in 1884 to take 450 pupils.

The church today has lost some of its pinnacles and now has a stone wall instead of railings. The school closed in 1953 when Witney Secondary School (now known as Wood Green School) opened.

F.O. Whitcher's at 29 High Street, dealer in flowers and provisions, existed until 1963, when three houses next to the shop were demolished to allow the construction of Welch Way.

Modernising and extending the buildings that were left on the new corner formed the present National Westminster Bank on the corner of High Street and Welch Way.

In the middle of the High Street, a horse and cart waits outside Meadowsweet stores owned by Goodwin Foster and Co. Ltd, grocers of 34 High Street, *c.* 1910. Next door is Alfred Usher's, stationer and bookseller of 32 High Street, the proprietor of which was J.J. Burford.

The changes to the road are quite dramatic, with a mini roundabout providing easy access to Welch Way and one of the town's car parks. Meadowsweet's stores is now occupied by the Bradford & Bingley Building Society and Alfred Usher's shop by Baker's the jewellers.

A view of High Street in flood, *c*. 1910. The building on the left with railings in front, partially obscured, is the old Congregational chapel. This and the adjoining cottages were pulled down in 1971, and a supermarket was built in its place.

High Street looking from the hill, showing Eaton's shop, Knight's machine printing works and the *Witney Gazette* offices, *c.* 1910.

Clarks and other modern retailers have moved in, their long shopfronts concealing the individuality of the surviving buildings.

C.W. List and Son, family butchers, 16 High Street, *c.* 1910. The owner proudly poses for this photograph along with the carcasses hanging outside the shop.

An altogether less spectacular street presence for the traders who replaced it, though the hamburger outlet keeps up the meat connection.

The building on the immediate left, at 1 High Street, was the head post office until recently. The shop two doors down belonged to Walker and Co. Stores Ltd, grocers, at no. 5.

The post office has now moved to new premises further up the hill on the same side, and Dentons Cycles have taken over the old post office building. The ivy has been removed. A road hump crossing has been added and Walker's premises are now occupied by Boots Opticians.

The building in the centre left of this early 1960s photograph was the doctor's house and surgery at the time. To its left is Hillside; to the right is the post office.

The doctor's house has given way to the new post office. Alongside is the new Lloyds Bank building; the bank was previously on Church Green.

CHAPTER SIX

MARKET SQUARE &
THE BUTTER CROSS

The fortnightly market, Market Square, c. 1910.

The Hill, a horse-drawn carriage outside the bank on the hill opposite the market square, 1904. To the left is Whitehead jewellers and beyond that the Marlborough Hotel. In addition to accommodation, the hotel offered stabling for horses.

The Midland Bank as it is today. Whitehead's shop has been taken over by the Woolwich Building Society, but little else has changed. During the war a brick air-raid shelter was built into the raised bank.

Market Square, 1900. At that time the Central Café was still the Temperance Hotel. Nearby was Cook and Boggis's tailor's shop; they had traded in Witney since 1898. They claimed to be London tailors, but provided a large range of services to the town including drapery, haberdashery and ladies' outfitting.

Boots occupies the Temperance Hotel premises and Boggis's shop, burnt into ruins, has long since disappeared. Initially it was replaced in the mid-1960s by a Waitrose supermarket. When this moved to new premises close by, the buildings were revamped to provide a shopping arcade.

Market Square, *c.* 1930. On the right is the Cross Keys public house; the Commercial Hotel and Boots are beyond.

Market Square cluttered with cars. Traffic-calming measures have been introduced to improve pedestrian safety.

Our first sight of the Market Square seen from the steps of the Marlborough Hotel, *c.* 1910. The shop on the right was Neave and Lea, chemist, druggist and optician, of 49 Market Square. The square at this stage was open to the High Street.

Mr Neave's former shop is clearly visible on the right of the picture, but it now sells china. The square has been paved and separated from the road, and still houses a modest market each Tuesday and Saturday. The square has had other uses: for example, in the 1960s it acted as a small car park.

Market Square, 1920s. On the far left is the Corn Exchange and on its right is the entrance to the Corn Exchange Yard which housed the Fire Brigade, Ambulance and West Oxfordshire District Council Depot, cattle market and mortuary. At that time there were fourteen voluntary staff to cover the Witney area. Next door is Rowley's, house furnishers, cabinet-makers and undertakers, at 21–9 Market Square.

Today the Market Square has been separated from the road with surrounding pavement and Rowley's shop has been replaced by the Co-op building. Changes can also be detected at the Corn Exchange, where the balcony and the railings have disappeared. The large building on the right is no longer operated by Oxford Motor Services Ltd but is a café.

The Town Hall seen from the war memorial, *c.* 1900. The tall building to the left of the Butter Cross is 25 Market Square and was occupied by the Pearl Assurance Company in the 1930s. This postcard was produced by Frank Packer, who was a well-known photographer from Chipping Norton.

The old buildings in the background of the top picture have largely disappeared and renovation work under the eaves to the Butter Cross is evident, taking away the Victorian decorative effect and returning it to more like its original form.

The Town Hall and shops viewed from the western side of Church Green. The Town Hall is a small but ancient stone building consisting of one large chamber, supported by nine columns, the lower stage forming an open piazza. Corn was once bought and sold there, and the building was occasionally used for lectures and other public events. The shops include Harris & Son, jeweller and clockmaker, and Joseph Stoddart, draper – names now long forgotten.

Traffic dominates the picture, and estate agents' premises now predominate in this part of the town. The buildings have undergone significant alteration and modernisation, and the roofline of the block has changed.

The Butter Cross, Town Hall and Market Square from the eastern side of Church Green, *c.* 1930. The Butter Cross was built in 1683 by William Blake of Cogges, and was renovated in 1811, 1868 and then the 1960s. It is a wooden structure supported by thirteen cylindrical pillars. It has four gables at the cardinal points, and at the apex of the roof is a square turret with an illuminated clock, paid for by subscription in 1889. The base was once used on market days for the sale of poultry, eggs, butter and other commodities.

Today the vista towards Church Green is virtually unchanged, except for alterations to keep traffic in its place.

The Butter Cross and, in the foreground to the right, the Electric Theatre, later known as the People's Palace, which opened in the 1920s. In the 1930s the times of opening were 5.45 p.m. until 10.15 p.m., and prices of admission to the stalls were 6*d*, 1*s*, 1*s* 3*d* and to the balcony 1*s* 6*d* and 1*s* 10*d*.

The former Crown Hotel building to the left of the Butter Cross has disappeared to allow the building of a road and new development, including the leisure centre by the River Windrush.

A close-up view of the Electric Theatre nearing completion. The cinema was built on the site of Fitze tailor's shop, which was destroyed by fire in 1909.

The Palace today, occupying the same site. The cinema showed its last film in 1985. The building has since been altered but it is still used for entertainment, now being a nightclub.

The rear of the old Crown Hotel, formerly a coaching inn. This was demolished in 1981 to form Langdale Gate.

Langdale Gate looking towards the Butter Cross and Corn Street. The tall building in the centre of this picture is the one to the left of the alley in the picture above. On the right, out of sight, is Langdale Hall, and beyond is Woolgate – part of the new shopping area.

A group of children poses for the photographer, *c*. 1910. Behind the Butter Cross is Leigh's shop. On the opposite corner is Tarrant's shop, 36 Market Square. The Tarrants were wholesale grocers and provision merchants, and had traded in Witney since 1869. In 1910 Mr E. Tarrant was the Council chairman.

The same view today finds only the Tarrant corner changed, to accommodate a new range of shops.

Leigh & Son ironmonger's shop, 38–40 Market Square. The shop has been owned and operated by the Leigh family for five generations. It remained unchanged until 1978 when Ian Leigh had the shop modernised.

No room to display the latest ironmongery in the roadway these days, but with the addition of further sons Leigh's business continues.

CHAPTER SEVEN

CORN STREET

Eastern end of Corn Street in the 1920s.

Tarrant's shop and warehouse, on the corner of Corn Street and opposite the Town Hall, under demolition in the 1960s. Originally the Lamb Inn was demolished to build Tarrant's shop.

Replacing Tarrant's is an undistinguished new building, which offers plenty of retail space.

Corn Street from the Butter Cross, 1953. On the left is the Red Lion public house; on the right the premises of H. Harris and Sons, confectioner and tobacconist, at no. 12.

New shops have appeared on the left and new building continues to spread up from Tarrant's corner on the right. The road entrance has been narrowed for safety.

Upper Corn Street looking towards the Butter Cross, free of traffic except for a couple of carts, 1907. On the immediate left is the Primitive Methodist chapel, which was built in 1869.

The same view today. The background to the picture has changed: the Crown Hotel is no longer there and the road that runs down towards the leisure centre and Cogges is visible.

The Swan Laundry (Witney) Ltd in Corn Street, 1960s. Their slogan was 'Let the Laundry do it all'. The shop was constructed in the space in front of the disused chapel.

The chapel restored to full view today. The Swan Laundry shop has been pulled down and replaced by steps to serve the chapel, which now houses a number of retail outlets.

Thomas Biles's shop, 32 Corn Street, 1960s. He was a builder, contractor in stone, marble and monumental mason and his family had occupied the premises since the 1860s.

The premises today show little change, apart from modest updating. Before they were occupied by Johnson's they housed an estate agent.

Lower Corn Street, showing on the left the premises of A.E. Horne, baker, 158–64 Corn Street, c. 1910. On the opposite side and slightly higher up the road was the Corn Street stores, at no. 117, which was operated by W.H. Tarrant and Sons who also had premises close to Market Square. They sold groceries and bacon.

Horne's premises have been taken over by M.A. Wilkins and converted to a car showroom. The shop at no. 17 now sells antiques rather than bread.

Corn Street (at the junction with the roads leading to Burford, Curbridge and Ducklington) and Witney cemetery, *c.* 1910. The land, originally a quarry, was purchased in 1857 for the sum of £170. It would appear that postcards were produced of any subject!

A roundabout, necessary to deal with the traffic at this busy junction which now includes Welch Way, dominates the picture. Welch Way replaced Dark Lane.

CHAPTER EIGHT

CHURCH GREEN

Witney Feast, Church Green, c. 1910.

Church Green and children at play, June 1903. The green at that time was also used for the feast fair. The event was only transferred to the Leys, behind St Mary's Church, in later years.

The picture taken in March 1998 shows the green looking quite different but this is mainly because the trees are not in leaf. Children now tend to play in the Leys, beyond St Mary's Church.

Church Green from the eastern side, with sheep grazing, 1905. A coach takes passengers from the railway station to the Fleece Hotel.

Grazing would not be possible today because of the volume of traffic. Church Green continues to be used for community events like the bi-annual trade fair.

The grammar school, Church Green, winter 1924. The school was founded in 1663 by Henry Box, citizen and grocer of London and native of Witney. Originally it took just thirty boys from the parish, but was reconstituted in 1877 as a co-educational school. It was taken over by the County Council in 1939.

Henry Box School as it is today. It has been significantly expanded with new buildings and now has over 1,200 pupils. Regrettably most of the original trees, which were elms and provided a noble approach to the school, became old and rotten and were removed in the 1970s.

A closer view of the school, which originally occupied a 2 acre site. The main building was built in stone, and provided residences at either end for the head and second masters. At the turn of the century the headmaster was the Revd Mr Pinder MA.

The site today. Queen Elizabeth, the Queen Mother, visited the school in 1963 on the occasion of its tercentenary. She arrived by helicopter, landing on Church Green.

The police station was erected on the west side of the Church Green in 1860 at a cost of £2,500. It had a large room in which petty sessions were held, and also included housing for an inspector and a sergeant, guard-rooms and cells. This postcard dates from 1933.

The building's exterior has changed very little but its use has. It now houses a number of County Council educational units, and the buildings to the left have been replaced to provide additional accommodation for Henry Box School. The police station is now in Welch Way.

The Mount House gateway, opposite the Almshouses, adjacent to St Mary's Church. It had been decorated to celebrate the coronation of King George VI on 12 May 1937. This is the site of the Bishop of Winchester's Palace which disappeared many years ago, the foundations having only been discovered recently. The private house was used as a hostel for the Women's Land Army during the Second World War.

The gateway today looks far less elegant. Mount House is no longer a private residence, but houses the Social Services Department of Oxfordshire County Council. New development is evident to the left.

The western side of Church Green, *c.* 1900, before the war memorial was erected.

The western side today. The war memorial in the foreground was unveiled on 12 September 1920. It commemorates the men connected with the district who lost their lives in the First World War. All the religious organisations in the town were present at the unveiling. The stone pillars and chains, and the names of Witney people who lost their lives in the Second World War, were added in the 1940s.

The war memorial from Church Green, *c*. 1925. Behind the bus are the Bull Inn, the Angel public house and Saltmarsh and Druces's shop, originally a grocer, wine and spirit merchant, tobacconist and medicine vendor. The shop is still there today.

Cars now dominate the picture: they have had a significant impact on Church Green.

The eastern side of Church Green, 1915. On the right is St Mary's National School, which was established in 1813 for 450 children. The average attendance over the years was 145 boys, 112 girls and 95 infants. Beyond is the Fleece Hotel.

At first glance little has altered. St Mary's School and the Fleece Hotel remain, but in fact the uses of most of the other buildings have changed.

CHAPTER NINE

THE LEYS &
RAILWAY STATION

The original terminus station at Witney, c. 1960.

The tree-lined walk at The Leys, 1920s. The park gates, railings and gas lamps have long since disappeared.

The park today. On the left and in the background there is clear evidence of the town's expansion, although The Leys maintains much of its original charm.

The Leys, sometimes known as Church Leys, was purchased in the 1920s as a public recreation ground with funds subscribed by Witney people in memory of those who lost their lives during the First World War.

The park continues to be used for recreational purposes and cricket is often played. The Leys also acts as host to the Witney Feast fair in September.

The new premises of the Witney Blanket Co. Ltd on The Leys, occupied in 1921. The company, believed to have been started in 1885, moved here from premises in Market Square.

The buildings remain but the use has changed: they are now a retail outlet.

St Mary's Church from the railway bridge, *c.* 1900. Beyond are Church Green and the town.

It has not been possible to take today's picture from exactly the same spot but the scene has changed significantly. On the left behind the wall The Leys remains but on the right there has been considerable development on the site once occupied by the railway.

Witney station, adjacent to The Leys and south of the Bowling Green, 1920. This picture shows all that remains of the original terminus. The station was opened by the Witney Railway Company in November 1861 and closed to passengers on 15 January 1873. It continued to be used as a railway-served goods depot until it finally closed on 2 November 1970. After closure it continued in use as Marriott's Coal Yard.

During 1996 the site was redeveloped and the new Sainsbury's supermarket built, seen here in 1998.

Witney station was the main station on the branch. This picture shows the new station which was opened on 15 January 1873 when the Witney Railway was extended through to Fairford by the East Gloucestershire Railway Company. Passenger services were withdrawn between Oxford and Fairford on 18 June 1962 and the station was closed. Here, a train hauled by a Great Western 'Queen' class 2–2–2 arrives from Fairford.

Unfortunately there is now no obvious reference point for the above picture, but take my word for it, this is the same place! The building is used by the Post Office and forms part of the Station Industrial Estate.

CHAPTER TEN

THE VILLAGES & TOWNS AROUND WITNEY

Ramsden Church.

The railway station at Alvescot, 8½ miles south-west of Witney, 1934. On the platform is a typical East Gloucestershire Railway stone station building and pagoda waiting room. The siding served as a coal yard.

The same spot today shows little evidence of a railway, although there is still a coal yard here. The latter is served by road.

Brize Norton and Bampton station, 4 miles south-west of Witney, May 1959. It was situated alongside Brize Norton airfield and was opened as Bampton station in 1873, being enlarged and renamed Brize Norton and Bampton on 1 May 1940.

Today the site is covered by a small industrial estate. The perimeter fence of the airfield can be seen on both pictures.

Carterton station, 7½ miles south-west of Witney, 1953. This was the next station along the line after Brize Norton and Bampton. It was opened by the Great Western Railway on 10 August 1944 to deal with the increase in service traffic to the nearby airfield. The station was actually closer to Black Bourton than Carterton.

The road bridge is the only feature that identifies the site today. The trackbed leads to a farm and the road across the bridge terminates at the airfield.

The Fish House, Cokethorpe, 2½ miles south of Witney, close to Ducklington, *c.* 1910. Opposite the Fish House is Cokethorpe Park, which contains a mansion built in 1711. For some time the mansion was the home of the poet John Gray.

The Fish House today. The ivy has disappeared from the building and a number of windows have been added.

Combe, sometimes known as Long Combe, 6 miles north-east of Witney, 1904. A number of people, including the postman, pose for the photographer. The village is bounded on the south by the River Evenlode, with Blenheim Park on the east. The Duke of Marlborough was the lord of the manor and principal landowner.

Very little has changed, although the horse and cart has inevitably been replaced by the motor car.

The Green, Combe, *c*. 1908. Again a number of people have been drawn by the photographer and are included in the picture. The original site of the village is said to have been in the adjoining valley of Evenlode: the mounds by the mill probably mark the ancient church.

The ancient tree which dominated the green has gone and the three cottages in the centre of the picture have been altered and combined to provide larger homes.

St Bartholomew's Church, Ducklington, 2 miles south-west of Witney. The church, built in a mixture of styles, was renovated and restored in 1872 and then again ten years later. The parochial school (left of picture) catered for both boys and girls. In 1869 the Mistress was Miss Emmeline Toombs.

The trees have grown and partly obscure the church and the houses behind it. The pond remains an important feature in the centre of the village.

Eynsham station. Ex-Great Western Railway metro tank no. 3562 stands at the down platform, 25 September 1948. The train went on from here to Fairford in Gloucestershire.

Another view of the trading estate, which now incorporates the fire station. The wartime platform from the station was removed from the site in 1984 and has since been reassembled at Didcot Railway Centre.

The Wesleyan Chapel at Hailey, 2 miles north of Witney, was built in 1908 and served the outlying hamlets of Delly End, Poffley End, White Oak Green and part of New Yatt.

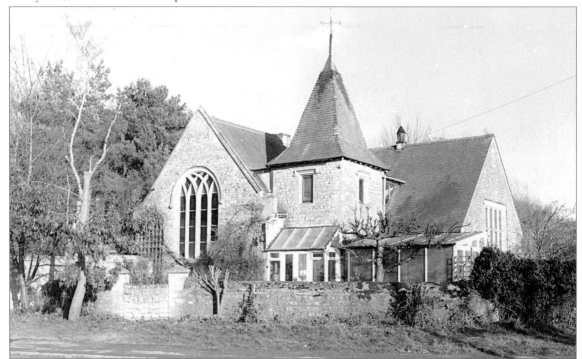

The chapel has been sympathetically converted into a comfortable home.

Long Hanborough, 8½ miles north-east of Witney, *c.* 1910. A group of people find time to pose for the photographer. It was a thriving village, which had a church, two chapels, two schools and a railway station.

The road and motor car dominate the picture. The wall has disappeared to provide access to the Bell Inn and its car park. Unlike in the other towns and villages around Witney, the railway station survives at Long Hanborough and provides an alternative to road transport for people travelling to Oxford.

Minster Lovell, 2¼ miles north-east of Witney, 1920. Close to the village is Charterville, which was an allotment estate containing eighty small farms of 2, 3 and 4 acres, each with a single-storey cottage. The estate was laid out in 1847 as part of Feargus O'Connor's Chartist land scheme.

Much of the village charm remains, and although changes are obvious, they have not materially affected this delightful place.

The ruins at Minster Lovell, 2¾ miles north-west of Witney. St Kenelm's Church and the ancient mansion (now in ruins) near to the River Windrush were built by Lord William Lovell between 1425 and 1465. The buildings originally formed a quadrangle. The only portions left standing are the north side, part of a tower, the south end of the western side and a low wall attached to it, with several fine but now roofless and dismantled apartments.

The site today shows little change, although the large tree, some of the wall and the gates have disappeared.

The Rose Revived public house at Newbridge, 7 miles south-east of Witney, *c.* 1905. The horse and cart belonged to William Johnson, a carrier from Standlake. He was also a millwright and ran the post office.

This photograph clearly shows how the building has been extended over the decades. In the last ten years it has changed from a gracious country hotel to a modern pub.

The Maybush Inn at Newbridge, c. 1910. This is an early photograph of the inn, which stands on the opposite side of the river to the Rose Revived. Note the boats and the people relaxing in the gardens of the inn.

The Thames continues to attract many visitors particularly in the summer, and the gardens have been equipped to cope with this. This pub has undergone some updating and additional buildings have been added. Regrettably most of the trees have disappeared from this garden.

North Leigh, 4 miles north-east of Witney, *c.* 1910. The village landmark is the windmill, which sadly stands derelict today. At East End, which is about 1 mile north-east, a Roman villa was discovered in 1814; it contains an interesting tessellated pavement.

At first glance little may appear to have changed, but significant development has taken place in various areas of the village since the previous picture was taken.

St Mary's Church, North Leigh, *c.* 1930. Originally cruciform, this is an interesting building in the Norman, Early English and Decorated styles. The tower is reported to be part Saxon and the clock, which was added in 1896, was a present from Miss Susannah Gascoigne of Ealing.

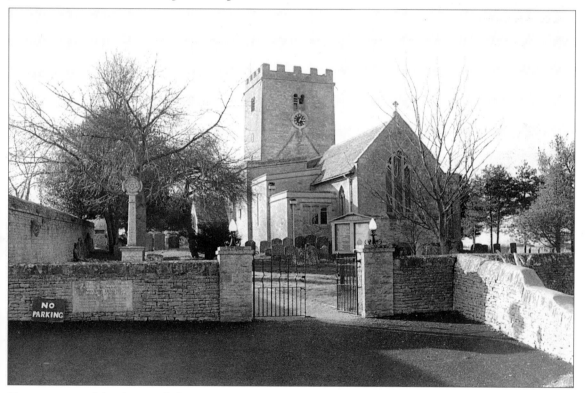

Close inspection of the photograph shows additional buildings on the left of the church. The wooden fence and gate have been replaced by a wall, and a wrought-iron gate and a notice-board have been added.

Northmoor, 7 miles south-east of Witney, *c.* 1910. The church of St Denys dates from the period between the early English and Decorated styles. The interior was restored and the church re-opened on 12 April 1887.

The horse and cart gives way to the motor car. Horses remain in the village, but more for recreation. New housing has been provided and modernisation is evident from the road signs and power poles.

The dovecot at Northmoor, *c.* 1920. At Bablock Hythe, about 1½ miles north-east of Northmoor, the river could be crossed by ferry. This provided easy access to Cumnor and significantly shortened the trip to Oxford.

The dovecot today remains unchanged, but the building behind it has been sympathetically converted into a home.

South Leigh station, 2½ miles south-east of Witney, *c.* 1959. It consisted of a single platform and a small wooden booking office, probably dating from the opening of the station in 1861. A level crossing stood at the Oxford end of the station, and the siding in the background served the Second World War cold store seen in the centre of the picture.

Today a house, aptly named South Leigh Station, has been constructed over the trackbed, and the old foodstore building, although long closed, remains.

The post office at South Leigh, 1920s. When this picture was taken Herbert Green was the sub-postmaster, and letters went via Witney, which was the nearest telegraph office. Money orders were provided by Stanton Harcourt post office.

The village retains much of its charm today.

The Golden Balls, Standlake, about 5 miles south-east of Witney. The photograph shows the workers of Charles W. Sirets about to embark on the employees' annual 'beanfeast' on 10 October 1910.

The site today. The pub was pulled down recently and a new prestige housing development put in its place.

The Harcourt Arms at Stanton Harcourt, 5 miles south-east of Witney, *c.* 1900. The landlord was Charles Askers, who was also a farmer and miller.

The Harcourt Arms today. The magnificent tree and some of the original buildings have disappeared. The modernisation has provided extensive parking for cars and accommodation for guests.

Stanton Harcourt, church and mansion, *c.* 1910. The photograph is a postcard by Henry Taunt, an Oxford photographer of considerable talent. The mansion house has been the family home of the Harcourts for 750 years. In the grounds is Pope's Tower. Alexander Pope, the poet, stayed at the house in the early eighteenth century and while there translated Homer's *Iliad*. The church to the left of the mansion is St Michael's and dates back to the twelfth century.

At first glance very little appears to have changed. There has been limited development in the village, but it still retains much of its charm.

Some of the five cottages in Stanton Harcourt, which formed part of the Harcourt Estate. The principal landowners at that time were, however, the University of Oxford, All Souls and Brasenose Colleges and the vicar.

Time seems to have stood still in this beautiful corner of West Oxfordshire.